Do You Feel Like a
Fraud?

Felicia M. Johnson

Typhanie
Investing in yourself
leads to success!
Felicia M.
Johnson
Apr 13, 2018

Dedication

This book is dedicated to those

who experienced Impostor Syndrome,

but didn't know what to call it.

Contents

- Remove your limiting beliefs
- Gather feedback from others
- Create your own highlight reel
- Create a playlist of songs
- Project your power
- Take care of your whole person
- Promote yourself confidently
- Pause and say "thank you"
- Provide support and seek support

Acknowledgements

Thank you to God for His grace and mercy!

Thank you to my husband, Trapper, for his emotional and financial support. The truck is on its way!

Thank you to my kids, Gabriel and Arielle, for understanding when I couldn't kick it with them as long on book writing days.

Thank you to my mom, Beulah, for always being open to read what I've written.

Thank you to my dad, Fredrick, who always believes I'm "twice as good."

Thank you to Janel, Tanisha, and Julie who used their awesome professional skills to get this book in your hands.

And…

Thank you for purchasing this book and having the courage to grapple with Impostor Syndrome. After reading it, I would greatly appreciate your review on Amazon.com

Introduction

·····················

"Investing in yourself leads to success."

–Felicia M. Johnson, *Success Coach*

"Every time I was called on in class, I was sure that I was about to embarrass myself. Every time I took a test, I was sure that it had gone badly. And every time I didn't embarrass myself—or even excelled—I believed that I had fooled everyone yet again. One day soon, the jig would be up . . . This phenomenon of capable people being plagued by self-doubt has a name—the Impostor Syndrome.

–Sheryl Sandberg, *COO of Facebook*

"Ah, the Impostor Syndrome!? The beauty of the Impostor Syndrome is you vacillate between extreme egomania, and a complete feeling of: 'I'm a fraud! Oh god, they're on to me! I'm a fraud!' So you just try to ride the egomania when it comes and enjoy it, and then slide through the idea of fraud. Seriously,

I've just realized that almost everyone is a fraud, so I try not to feel too bad about it."

–Tina Fey, *actress, comedian*

"What's it called when you have a disease and it keeps recurring? I go through [acute Impostor Syndrome] with every role. I think winning an Oscar may in fact have made it worse. Now I've achieved this, what am I going to do next? What do I strive for? Then I remember that I didn't get into acting for the accolades, I got into it for the joy of telling stories."

–Lupita Nyong'o, *actress*

· · · · · · · · · · · · · · · · · ·

As a parent, what you name your child is extremely important. Why? Names call us forth, right? That child named "Moon Unit" will likely have a different destination from the one named "Harold." Names designate a slice of future identity.

My husband and I named our daughter Arielle.

And no—not like the mermaid.

Arielle is a biblical name meaning "Lioness of God." Packed within it, I've read, are traits like the following: *Loves life and adventure. Very intelligent, but doesn't show off her smarts. Loves to protect the underdog. Very kind and giving selflessly. Can champion a cause if she believes it is good.*[1]

We characterize lions as the king of the land. They are respected, powerful, and courageous. My husband and I crave all of these traits for our daughter and every day we're slowly and purposefully investing in this purpose.

And in this, we're intentionally laying brick after brick to create a foundation that will thwart what statistically, she along with an estimated 70 percent of other people, will experience; at least one episode of Impostor Syndrome.[2]

Surprisingly, it's successful people—those defying common boundaries—who are most likely to exhibit Imposter Syndrome on a regular bases. Despite your outer stature as king of the jungle, you experience internal self-doubt and criticism that makes you feel more like Tigger. Or Hello Kitty.

What if I told you that instead of this crippling inferiority, you could swell into the confidence of a lioness, stalking for food for her pride?

C'mon. Let's get started matching your outer lioness with your inner one.

---

[1]http://www.urbandictionary.com/define.php?term=arielle
[2]http://bsris.swu.ac.th/journal/i6/6-6_Jaruwan_73-92.pdf+

PART 1
···················
Fraud … Is that You?

The date is February 26, 2017. It's a night dripping with camera flashes, couture gowns, tailored tuxedos, red carpets, and legends of the silver screen clustered together to learn if they have won a gold statue named "Oscar". It's the Academy Awards Ceremony.

Viola Davis added her scarlet Armani gown to the rich froth of color. Now nominated for Best Supporting Actress for her role alongside Denzel Washington in the movie *Fences*, she was not unfamiliar with tonight's flamboyant clamor. She had been nominated twice before.

Tonight, Viola would win the Oscar—and to many, would validate her stature as one of the greats. She is the first and only Black woman to be nominated for three Academy Awards, and is the first and only black actress to win the Triple Crown of Acting. Her stirring connection with audiences was confirmed by host Jimmy Kimmel's commentary on her acceptance: "Viola Davis just got nominated for an Emmy for that speech!"

Later, an interviewer questioned Viola. How was she feeling about her win?

She responded, *"I just wanted to be good at something. And so this is sort of like the miracle of God, of dreaming big and just hoping that it sticks and it lands, and it did. Who knew? So I'm overwhelmed. Yeah."* To me, watching from home, finally unwinding after work in my sweats, she sounded like a woman who had worked hard at her craft, used her God-given abilities, and was simply humbled to acquire the Oscar.

In another interview later that evening, Viola confirmed she had worked hard, yet she revealed something else that intrigued me. She said, *"It feels like my hard work has paid off, but at the same time I still have the **impostor...syndrome**. I still feel like I'm going to wake up and everybody's going to see me for the hack I am. I still feel like when I walk on the set, I'm starting from scratch, until I realize, OK, I do know what I'm doing. I'm human."*

Those two, simple words—"Impostor Syndrome"—neatly labels the phenomenon burrowing deeply inside the majority of the world's population. Viola's not the only one questioning her legitimacy.

I'm a hack.

I still can't believe they're letting me do this!

They're on to me.

It's only a matter of time before they find me out.

I'm a fraud.

I'm such a fake.

I just got lucky.

I don't belong.

Anyone could have done that.

I can't afford to fail.

It's because they like me—not because I deserve it.

They must have made a mistake picking me.

It's only because of my connections.

I fooled them again.

I don't deserve to be here.

I don't know how I pulled that off.

When was the last time you made one of these statements, even there in the cobwebbed corners of your mind?

You're not the only one.

To begin coaching others through Impostor Syndrome, I began sharing information on my Instagram and Facebook accounts (@fsocareercoach). This is a quote I posted by Emma Watson, winner of the Young Artist Award for Leading Young Actress for her performance in *Harry Potter and the Sorcerer's Stone*:

> *It's almost like the better I do, the more my feeling of inadequacy actually increases, because I'm just going, Any moment, someone's going to find out I'm a total fraud, and that I don't deserve any of what I've achieved. I can't possibly live up to what everyone thinks I am and what everyone's expectations of me are. It's weird.*

The first responses to my post were:

Sally*: THIS!!!!

Mary*: I LITERALLY just said the words "it makes me feel like a fraud" to my husband not 30 minutes ago. What fantastic timing to open Facebook and see this so soon! Thanks!

Mary*: Ha! And John* just said "I'm glad you read that" when I showed it to him. So thanks again!

Impostor Syndrome (also called Impostor Phenomenon) was described in 1978 by Drs. Pauline R. Clance and Suzanne A. Imes. The concept describes people who have intense feelings that their successes are undeserved and worry that they will be exposed

---

* Names Changed

as frauds, which causes them distress, anxiety, and self-sabotaging behavior.

If unchecked, Impostor Syndrome can cause fear, anxiety, stress, loss of confidence, procrastination, quitting, shying away from attention, concealing your opinions, and self-sabotage.

Common indicators:

✓ You have difficulty accepting compliments and recognition.

✓ You feel you need to work twice as hard to prove you're worthy.

✓ You avoid situations where you're not 100% confident you know what you are doing. (And asking for help feels a little like that naked-in-the-mall dream.)

✓ In your lack of confidence, you procrastinate until the last minute to work on assignments.

✓ When you succeed, you doubt you could repeat it again—any success, after all, is like snow in Los Angeles; Highly unlikely, and if so, something is up.

✓ Everything has to be perfect before revealing a project you have been working on.

✓ You worry regularly about your performance, fearing you won't meet people's expectations and being uncovered as a fraud.

Hear me out. You are not, statistically speaking, an impostor. A "real impostor" is someone who pretends to be able to do something or have specific skills, despite not actually possessing the skills, background or experience.

History is full of true impostors. Guys like Ferdinand Demara, who impersonated a naval surgeon and Frank Abagnale, source of inspiration for the film *Catch Me If You Can*, who assumed no less than eight identities, including an airline pilot, physician, and lawyer. Unless you're fooling all of us about your background, skills, or experience — a fraud, that's not you!

Impostor Syndrome is not just another word for low self-esteem. Remember, Impostor Syndrome is a trait of people who have acquired some success and are viewed as having attained achievement in some form of fashion.

If that whisper in your mind just piped up, "Aha! See? I don't view myself as successful"—this self-discovery book is definitely for you! I'm here to help you slough off that confining skin that handicaps us into underachievement—and prevents you from fully serving those around you due to a complex series of subtle, crippling lies.

Now, don't freak out. Impostor Syndrome isn't some form of mental disorder. This is simply an ingrained reaction to certain situations. You most likely experience it after a notable accomplishment such as

- Earning that promotion for which you've been working overtime all last year.

- Winning the award for that out-of-the-box marketing campaign you put together.

- Landing that job, despite missing a few of the qualifications they listed.

- Launching (at last) that new business you've meticulously researched or creatively cobbled together.

- Writing that book that's been hunching in the back of your mind for months—or maybe years?

Impostor Syndrome is as common as a melting popsicle on the Fourth of July. Impostor Syndrome isn't picky. It can affect anyone. But if you're a woman or a minority, you're particularly vulnerable.

Did you just see me raise my hand? Yep. This book is a product of my own self-discovery, clawing my way out of the trenches dug by my past experiences and assumptions. I too scrabble with Impostor Syndrome. You'll be reading how my impostor spoke her lambaste voice —even while authoring the book in your hands.

As your coach, I will provide resources and tips to help tackle the inner critic crouching within you. I approach this book not merely as a researcher or a pharmacist (Take this! You'll feel better!)—but as a woman who, like Viola Davis, still must address the voice in my head who scoff at hard-won triumphs

In the midst of my advice, I'll relate openly how this syndrome has at times cannibalized me as a wife, mom, Black woman, Christian, and career professional.

But it's more than that.

It's also how I—and you—can overcome.

Throughout this book you'll see this icon.

It's a heads up for you to take some form of action to give Impostor Syndrome a sucker-punch. So don't just glide over these, like it's a chore akin to sweeping the floor. I'm extending to you an opportunity to tangibly address the accumulated junk in your brain—and replace those "ingrained patterns" with new, life-giving habits of body and spirit.

Dr. Pauline Clance developed a twenty-question scaled rating assessment called the Clance Impostor Phenomenon Scale. It helps people self-discover whether or not they have impostor characteristics and, if so, to what extent they suffer. Below are five sample questions that may not be fully representative of the 20-item scale.[3]

1. I have often succeeded on a test or task even though I was afraid that I would not do well before I undertook the task.

---

[3]The Impostor Phenomenon: When Success Makes You Feel Like A Fake (pp. 20-22), by P.R. Clance, 1985, Toronto: Bantam Books. Copyright 1985 by Pauline Rose Clance, Ph.D., ABPP. Reprinted by permission.

2. I can give the impression that I'm more competent than I really am.

3. I avoid evaluations if possible and have a dread of others evaluating me.

4. When people praise me for something I've accomplished, I'm afraid I won't be able to live up to their expectations of me in the future.

5. I sometimes think I obtained my present position or gained my present success because I happened to be in the right place at the right time or knew the right people.

Here's your first action step. Let's discover just how much Impostor Syndrome impacts your life.

Find a place and time that would allow you to take this assessment with limited distractions. Visit Dr. Pauline Clance's website and take her online assessment at http://paulineroseclance.com/impostor_phenomenon.html[4]

---

[4]Due to the ever changing speed of the internet, if you visit this site and the address has changed, simply search for Clance Impostor Phenomenon Scale.

·················

"Because your subconscious mind believes everything you say, nothing is more important than what you say to yourself."

– Anonymous

·················

PART 2

Where Impostor Syndrome Resides—In Your Mind

Confession: I'm a sucker for a great "overcome the odds" romance movie. Throw in some popcorn and snuggle with my husband, and you've got a lovely Friday night. One of my favorite flicks: *The Last Dragon*. (Yes, the one made in 1985. Seriously, I like it!) It begins with Leroy, a Kung Fu student, and his teacher performing a concentration exercise as Leroy muscles through a course of apparatus.

Simultaneously, his teacher flings arrows at him with a small bow.(No one said starring in a Kung Fu movie would be easy.) Leroy's task is to Karate chop down the arrows distinguished by a small piece of red tape.

He is to catch the single arrow labeled with blue tape. (I know! Piece of cake, right?)

In a moment, Leroy is amazed: He caught the blue one.

Leroy's Teacher: How did you know that was the Blue one?

Leroy: I do not know, Master.

Leroy's Teacher: You do not know?

(Leroy drops to his knees.)

Leroy: I humbly apologize for my ignorance, Master. I will do anything to prove my worthiness!

Leroy's Teacher: You have been to the movies again, I see, full of disciples falling to their knees at the slightest hint of their master's displeasure. . . . Leroy, this is not a punishment, it is a celebration: You have touched the final level. You knew *without knowing*. We have finished our journey together. (emphasis added)

Impostor Syndrome, operating in your conscious and unconscious mind, is derived from ingrained patterns. We can reform those patterns so that we might *know without knowing* that we are, in fact, just as qualified as God intricately orchestrated our lives to be!

Throughout life, we progress to levels where we're unconscious of our competence: from walking or tying our shoes, to driving or spelling, to regularly cooking dinner for our families. We haven't always known these skills—and yet now, we perform them without thinking.

Let's fully examine this with Noel Burch's Four Stages of Competence.

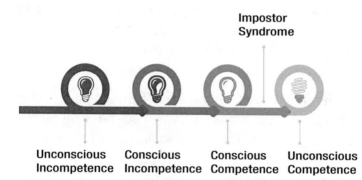

Unconscious incompetence – You do not understand or know how to do something and do not recognize the skill as important.

Conscious incompetence – You do not understand or know how to do something, *but* recognize the deficit and the value of acquiring the skill.

Conscious competence – You understand or know how to do something. However, executing the skill requires conscious effort and *concentration*.

Impostor Syndrome – You have intense feelings that your successes are undeserved and worry that they will be exposed as a fraud.

Unconscious competence – You perform a skill efficiently and it has become "second nature" or "automatic". At this level, you can possibly teach it to others.

Let's unpack this using a girl named Tiffany and her journey from opening her first lemonade stand to senior marketing executive.

Tiffany's mom held a garage sale and Tiffany decided she would open a lemonade stand. Her mom suggested she create a poster board to advertise and attract buyers. She also suggested for Tiffany to read *The Lemonade War*. During the garage sale, Tiffany was standing on the corner waving a poster board, drawing in customers to her lemonade sale.

Until her mom gave her the idea of creating the poster and reading the book, Tiffany had no clue about marketing. That's unconscious incompetence. (You didn't even know you were clueless, actually. But now, you're educated.) By reading the book, Tiffany entered into conscious incompetence. She was eager to learn.

Eight years later, the lemonade stand girl has a degree in marketing and was hired as a product account manager. Her first year at the soft drink company is a whirlwind of her working her tail off just to keep up with the jargon the rest of the team throws around like confetti. She refers to old textbooks and the company's example marketing plans to make sure she crosses every *"t"* and dots every *"i"*. At this point, she is competent—but consciously competent.

But give it a few years, and she's the expert at the table, educating the newbies. No one has to tell her how to evaluate target audiences or demographics or SEO terms. She just knows what to do. Ta-*da*: Without even realizing it, she glided across the threshold into unconscious competence.

I reason that Impostor Syndrome lives within the levels of conscious competence and unconscious competence. When people are able to complete something easily and without much thought, those experiencing Impostor Syndrome may begin to feel like a fraud. They may believe that because something no longer requires their conscious effort, they're playing the system somehow. They could also feel like an impostor because they are familiar with others' performance and view everyone else (but themselves, that is) as an expert.

Consider the professional skill sets you *currently* have. List them below.

Consider the professional skill sets you desire to acquire. List them below.

Consider each one. On which level of competence or incompetence would you place each one?

Do you have any unconscious competence-level skills which you discount because you no longer have to "work" at them?

Do you have any conscious competence-level skills which you discount because you don't yet feel fluent in them?

Are you struggling to determine what your skills are?

It's okay. I've been there too. In the past I used to feel like I was not an "expert" at anything! I would think—and even say—I am a B+ in a lot of different areas, but not an A in anything. The one thing I did allow myself to entertain was critiquing situations... or people... and assessing how they could be improved. But sharing that would make me seem negative, critical, or even judgmental. Who wanted to hang out with a person like that?

As a person who was expected to make all A's, feeling like a B+ person never set well with me. This brown woman just felt vanilla; plain and basic.

We disservice ourselves if the only source of our value is to be like everyone else. No one—not a one—is skilled in every area and that's okay. Linda Slaton, author of *Embracing Purpose*, once shared with me that each of us have both a shared purpose and a specific purpose. Our shared purpose: to bring glory to God. Our specific purpose is how we uniquely accomplish that.

You should choose to invest in areas in which you're specifically gifted or interested, or which offer salient expertise to your team. A great resource to help you identify, understand, and maximize your strengths is the CliftonStrengths assessment created by Don Clifton.[5]

The assessment can help you discover, grow and succeed. Gallup, Inc. says *"People who use their strengths every day are six times more likely to be engaged in their work and three times more likely to say they have an excellent quality of life."*

To allow you to get to know your coach better, I'll share with you just a couple of my top five signature themes—my strengths and a little bit about what makes me stand out in that area.

First—God made me a **relator**. That means I enjoy close relationships with others. Relators find deep satisfaction in working hard with friends to achieve a goal. More distinctively, I can pinpoint some of the unique likes, dislikes, strengths, limitations, work style, or experiences of particular people.

Can you see how this lends itself toward my unique

[5]https://www.gallupstrengthscenter.com/home/en-US/Index

position as a coach? Ephesians 2:10 reads, *"For we are his workmanship, created in Christ Jesus for good works, which God prepared beforehand, that we should walk in them"*. That word "workmanship"? Its original Greek counterpart is poiema, which is where we get the word *poem*. See where I'm going with this? We're expressions of God; his poem—each of us, an unrivaled expression. And in that expression, he's prepared good stuff for us to do. For me, that "relator" part of his knowledgeable craftsmanship of me empowers me to coach others well.

You can also see that in the part of me that is a **maximizer**. As a maximizer, I focus on strengths as a way to stimulate personal and group excellence. Maximizers seek to transform something strong into something superb. Even if I was a relator, without that maximizer—I'd be an ineffective coach.

Are you seeing how our strengths can dovetail beautifully into good works for God's honor—the particular works He has prepared for us?

What do you think your top five strengths could be?

If you took the CliftonStrengths assessment, what new discoveries or confirmations did you encounter?

PART 3

. . . .

Imposter syndrome—Why You?

By this point, you're now wondering, "Why am I like this? And where the heck did I get that?"

Valerie Young, Ed.D addresses this in her book, The Secret Thoughts of Successful Women: Why Capable People Suffer from the Impostor Syndrome and How to Thrive in Spite of It (2011). Here are a few, combined with my own:

You're not Tarzan.

. . . .

"It takes a village to raise a child."

–African Proverb

. . . .

You were not raised by animals, alone in the rainforest with only your own intuition. You had parents, teachers, coaches, and a host of other adults who molded your self-expectations. They shaped what you value, accept, and expect.

Many people with Impostor Syndrome were raised in families that placed a high emphasis on achieving success. A seed of Impostor Syndrome was planted one night in my middle-school years following a meal at a restaurant, the waiter handed my father the ticket. My dad with a lively gleam in his brown eyes, handed it to me and said it was for me to pay. Looking it over to see how much it was and if I could pay the bill, I noticed the line items did not add up correctly. I showed the error to my father, who confirmed my finding with a proud glance of approval. The waiter hurried off to correct the bill. From that day forth, I would always be given the bill to check for errors—and lovingly nicknamed by him "Brain"—the smart one.

My new nickname became intertwined with the eagerness to please and perform for a man I respected so greatly...admittedly along with the anxiousness to meet his often quite reasonable expectations of my intelligence. One afternoon when I proudly set before my dad a report card of all A's and one B, and my dad simply remarked, "What's up with the B?" The comment cemented in my mind that I must be the best in all areas—and caused me to be instantly self-conscious of anything that might be labeled by someone else as "B-level" work.

Combined with my personality, desires, interpretations, and choices, vignettes like these sculpted my identity. I need to accept responsibility for how I've responded to those around me, because blaming surrenders much of my capacity to change! No, we can't choose our influences. But our own responses—intentional and unintentional—to those influences can impact those "ingrained patterns."

You're a Woman.

....

"Think like a queen. A queen is not afraid to fail.

Failure is another steppingstone to greatness."

–Oprah Winfrey, *OWN network owner*

....

The Center for Talent Innovation reported women want five things in their career.[6] They are:

1. Flourish

2. Excel

3. Reach for meaning and purpose

4. Earn well

5. Empower others and be empowered

---

[6]http://www.talentinnovation.org/_private/assets/WomenWant%20 FiveThings_ExecSumm-CTI.pdf

Many female employees don't have it easy in the workplace. Experts reveal female employees repeatedly encounter bias throughout their careers. There is still an unspoken rule in some workplaces that women are not smart, weak, or inferior to men.

Gender Bias Against Women of Color in Science[7] was a study that surveyed 557 women and described five biases they face in the workplace.

1. Women have to prove themselves over and over again—their successes are discounted, their expertise questioned.

2. Women were expected to behave in a competent masculine manner but also expected to be feminine.

3. Women who have children have their commitment and competence questioned.

4. Women are forced to compete with each other, rather than support, for the coveted "woman's spot".

5. Women are mistaken for either administrative or custodial staff.

In 2017, a male engineer at Google authored a ten-page diversity manifesto. He claimed that biological differences made women less suited for careers in

[7]http://www.uchastings.edu/news/articles/2015/01/double-jeopardy-report.pdf

technology. Here's what he had to say about the biological differences.

> "I'm simply stating that the distribution of preferences and abilities of men and women differ in part due to biological causes and that these differences may explain why we don't see equal representation of women in tech and leadership".

Here is part of Google's CEO response to the manifesto:

> To suggest a group of our colleagues have traits that make them less biologically suited to that work is offensive and not OK . . . The memo has clearly impacted our co-workers, some of whom are hurting and feel judged based on their gender. Our co-workers shouldn't have to worry that each time they open their mouths to speak in a meeting, they have to prove that they are not like the memo states, being "agreeable" rather than "assertive," showing a "lower stress tolerance," or being "neurotic."

Once I was in a business meeting with two men whom I'll call Mark and David. Mark was the supervisor of a team member who'd dropped the ball on an event we were organizing. After explaining the chain of events and the action plan for recovering—and following my own explanation—David turned to Mark: "I don't understand." David proceeded to repeat my explanation. Sometimes, I realize that we simply need someone else to say things in a different way to us. But immediately, my mind had to wonder: Why was I being cut out of the conversation? Did this have to do with my gender? My race? (And was I being oversensitive in even considering my last two questions?)

You're a Black Woman

· · · · · · · · · · · · · · · · · · ·

"I didn't learn to be quiet when I had an opinion. The reason they knew who I was is because I told them."

–Ursula Burns, *Xerox Chairman & CEO*

· · · · · · · · · · · · · · · · · · ·

Double jeopardy? Being a woman of color often carries additional burdens imperceptible to those around us.

- Being perceived as too strong to need anybody's help or support

- Being viewed as mad or aggressive instead of assertive

- Being "invisible", their presence not recognized

- The perception that they were only hired because of affirmative action or a diversity innovative—not for their skills and other attributes they bring to the job

Let's explore that last point a bit. After working twice as hard to achieve their success, you can be confronted daily by others who think you don't belong because you lack the skills. They constantly doubt you or question your skills. After encountering that so many times, it can lead to you doubting and questioning yourself.

Lieutenant General Nadja West is the first female African-American three-star general in U.S. Army history, and the highest-ranking woman ever to graduate from West Point. During her career path, she had a conversation with one of her friends—not an enemy or hater, but a friend—who told her that the only reason she was being promoted through the ranks was because of her race and gender.

West shared,

> He goes, 'Well, you realize that, you know, the only reason that you got promoted is because you're an African-American female'. That's why I showed him my—we have this officer record brief. I was the distinguished undergraduate in my class of flight surgeon course. The top graduate.

Although she was able to stand up for herself and prove the basis for her success, she also felt,

> "If you told me when I was a plebe at West Point that you're going to be a three-star general, I

*would have laughed you out of the room because
I just didn't see it. I couldn't see it in myself."*

Today, Lt. Gen. West openly speaks about her past insecurities and how she has gained confidence. When she sees other women, she takes the time to encourage them on their journey.

I, too, can understand the struggles of maneuvering in a military environment. My dad served in the U.S. Army; our family moved often, from the South, to the East Coast, to Hawaii, and to international forts. In addition, a majority of my career was working as a civilian for the military. Each move brought new people and cultures, which often required emotional intelligence.

Read how Joyce Roche, author; President and CEO of Girls, Inc. described her workplace experience.

"The impostor fears had a greater impact on me early in my career. As I entered corporate America, I faced many unknowns. Being a woman of color in business at a time when very few women were in positions of power, I had to learn by trial and error how I was supposed to perform. This made me so afraid of being wrong or 'looking dumb' that I stayed quiet in meetings. I wanted to make sure everything I said was perfect before I would chance saying anything, and often found myself hearing a guy saying what I had been thinking but was too afraid to say."

A 2015 study performed by Center for Talent

Innovation[8] found that 87 percent of Black women want to be leaders, 81 percent want to achieve a high-ranking position, and 89 percent want to have stimulating work.

Perhaps you're thinking, *Of course they do. Is this unique to Black women?* Some studies would argue... yes. This study asserts,

> *On one critical front black and white women are extremely different. White women are reserved about wanting the top jobs in their organizations: they are uncertain about wielding power. Black women on the other hand are shooting for those top jobs.*

We're constantly—and at times subconsciously—evaluating the additional rules of the game Black women have to play. Those elusive leadership roles, to many of us feel like our golden ticket.

Many Black women are raised to believe they have to be "twice as good" to be viewed as successful.

The scene that played out on the popular TV show *Scandal* (2013) dipped into this reality comes to mind. Papa Pope carried out this conversation with his Black daughter, Olivia Pope:

Papa Pope: Did I not raise you for better?... How many times have I told you: You have to be *what*?

---

[8]http://www.talentinnovation.org/_private/assets/BlackWomenReady-ToLead_ExecSumm-CTI.pdf

Oliva: Twice.

Papa Pope: You have to be what?!

Oliva: Twice as good.

Papa Pope: Twice as good as them to get half of what they have! ... God sakes! You know to aim higher. At the very least, you could aim for chief of staff, secretary of state — first lady!? Do you have to be so mediocre?

Whew! The first time I saw this scene on the show...I cried. I connected deeply, perhaps painfully so, with so many young Black women who maintain this expectation placed on us by others.

What do people expect of me? Do I need to respect that to stay out of trouble...or work harder to blow those expectations out of the water? If I blow it, will that be attributed to my race? My gender? Do I belong here?

You're a Christian Woman

....

"An excellent wife who can find?
She is far more precious than jewels."

–Proverbs 31:10

....

I already touched on how you may be susceptible to

Impostor Syndrome because you are a woman or a Black woman. But because I am a Christian, I also find additional challenges that feed my Impostor Syndrome.

Perfectionism is another sign of Impostor Syndrome. As Christians we strive to be more and more like Jesus, who was perfect in every way. He was without sin. When others know you are a Christian, they will view and hold you to what they perceive as the appropriate Christian behavioral standards. Jesus was a perfect example to help my spiritual and personal growth—not to condemn me during my learning process. Everyone has fallen short of the glory of God (Romans 3:23) and striving for holiness doesn't mean I have to be perfect.

However, there was another character in the Bible that I was comparing myself to. I had the sneaking suspicion I was being a phony Christian woman if I wasn't succeeding at life like the Proverbs 31 woman. I felt like a phony if others *thought* I was pulling it off, but remained clueless to the struggles I encountered on any given day in all the hats (wife, mom, career professional, business owner, and community leader) stacked on my curly hair.

The Proverbs 31 woman:

> *Works with willing hands . . . She rises while it is yet night and provides food for her household . . . She considers a field and buys it; with the fruit of her hands she plants a vineyard . . . She dresses*

*herself with strength and makes her arms strong
. . . She opens her hand to the poor and reaches
out her hands to the needy . . . She makes linen
garments and sells them . . . She opens her mouth
with wisdom, and the teaching of kindness is on
her tongue . . . does not eat the bread of idleness
. . .Her children rise up and call her blessed . . .*

My expectations to achieve perfectionism—now *that's* phony. We saddle ourselves with undue pressures to be perfect. Somehow, we believe that would be the only way to be accepted by our spouse, kids, co-workers, and God.

It's okay if I didn't get a chance to sew the button back on my husband's shirt, or put away all the clean clothes, or cooked dinner late, or didn't get to work out four times this week.

A friend of mine once wrote, "Rather than motivated by fear—of failure, weakness, not being accepted—*holiness is now motivated by faith that I am unconditionally, overwhelmingly loved, accepted, and thankfully not in control*" (emphasis added).

Thankfully Jesus was already perfect on my behalf.

---

[9]http://ymi.today/2017/08/stop-being-perfect-start-being-holy/

You're the First or Only

"If your actions create a legacy that inspires others to dream more, learn more, do more and become more, then, you are an excellent leader."

–Dolly Parton, *singer-songwriter*

As a high school student, I was fortunate to be apart of Distributive Education Clubs of America (DECA.) This program allowed me to have a part-time job while in school. When I would go to my job, my father's go-to line was "Remember who you represent." It was his caring way of reminding me I had a privilege and not to blow it.

When you're the first or only youth, female, minority, hard of hearing, person in a wheelchair, or immigrant at a company—you worry that if you do not perform, it will affect the next person trying to follow in the same path of access. You want to avoid behaving in a way that causes others to say, "We tried that already. It was a disaster."

You feel the pressure to represent well, because if you fail, you think they won't just say it was you, but also all others that are similar to you. Once you make it through the door, you feel the pressure not to mess up and block access for others to enter behind you.

When Laura Chinchilla was asked in an interview how she felt about being elected as Costa Rica's first female president, she said,

> *"You not only have to do it well, because leading a country is something quite important, but also because I am the first woman I have to do it the best possible way so my country can continue voting for women in the future. It is a big responsibility."*

You are not alone wanting to avoid making mistakes or appearing incompetent, which could possibly blow the opportunity for others with similar backgrounds.

You're Interviewing For or Starting a New Job

· · · · · · · · · · · · · · · · · · · ·

"It's perfectly okay to occasionally feel like a fraud when it comes to your career. I'm just not sure you need to say that on your resume."

–Mike Shapiro, *cartoonist*

· · · · · · · · · · · · · · · · · · · ·

Did you know that statistically speaking, men apply for a job when they meet only 60 percent of the qualifications—but women apply only if they meet 100 percent of them? So if you're a woman and you've landed that interview—my kudos to you!

Jitters are to be expected in any interview. Naturally,

it's a time of questions and answers and analysis of your past experiences. As women, we may sometimes sabotage ourselves during the interview because we feel like impostors. I also venture out to say it is because women are less likely to feel comfortable with self-promoting. Women often think it's not modest to brag about their accomplishments. However, men do it all the time and are seen as being confident.

It may also be related to your interpretation of Romans 12:3 *"For by the grace given to me I say to everyone among you not to think of himself more highly than he ought to think, but to think with sober judgment, each according to the measure of faith that God has assigned."*

You're a woman who just applied for a job which you considered "reaching" a bit. Of course you prepare in advance for the interview, constructing responses to questions that may arise about your deficiencies. In the end, your interviewer is impressed and hires you for the job, completely aware of the areas in which you need training. However, Impostor Syndrome hisses in your ear, *"You poser, you've fooled them into thinking you're qualified."*

You may even begin your job unconsciously sabotaging your performance with thoughts of insecurity and expectations to fail. You start your new job thinking "someone made a mistake in the hiring process." Encountering new challenges, procedures, and a work culture can leave you feeling inadequate or paralyzed; leading to act in fear of making a mistake or failing.

In considering whether or not my failure is an indicator of a norm, I consider a formula created by Colin Powell, American statesman and retired four-star general: P= 40-70

P stands for *probability of success*. The 40-70 range indicates the percentage of information needed to form a wise, educated decision. Once you hit between the 40-70 range, go with your gut. Powell advises you should not take action when you only have enough information to give you less than 40 percent chance of being right. But don't wait until you have enough facts to 100 percent sure. By then, it's almost always too late.

Everyone makes mistakes. Just because you didn't perform at the 100 percent level at everything you do does not mean you're a phony! Relax, relate, release!

You're an Entrepreneur

....

*"I wake up every morning and think to myself,
'How far can I push the company forward
in the next 24 hours?"*

–Leah Busque, *Entrepreneur and founder*

....

You essentially work alone with no one to help you see your blind spots or encourage you. It's easy for to be overtaken by self-doubt.

You build a business from scratch and it becomes successful. You think, *I don't know how I did it.* Or perhaps, *I'm just waiting for this baby to fail.* You live in constant anxiety of the future; of your weakness or failure to plan resulting in the sweet candy of your dreams turning to sour grapes in your mouth.

My parents were raised in lower-income families. My dad joined the Army in determination of his own family avoiding the same circumstances. The military provided a steady income and housing for us. Over time I was taught that working for the government was dependable and safe—and hence, that was what I should strive for in my career.

My first job out of college was working as a civilian for the Army. Because of the many years of conditioning, allowing myself to accept the risks not only of non-government jobs, but the higher uncertainty of entrepreneurship in my own coaching business—sat like a rock in my stomach. What was I doing, putting my finances, my hopes—would it be my family, too?—on the line?

You're a Student

·····················

*"Today, I feel much like I did when I came to
Harvard Yard as a freshman in 1999 ...
I felt like there had been some mistake—that I
wasn't smart enough...."*

–Natalie Portman, *actress*

·····················

As a student, your knowledge and skills are tested quite literally to determine if you measure up to the standards. Your grade is based on how many mistakes or errors you make. And as you're likely picking up by this point—many people with Impostor Syndrome struggle with the fear of making a mistake.

I grew up for years being known as "Brain"—so entering college as an honor student, I didn't feel too much out of my element. . . . Until I took accounting. It was the first class I received a "C" grade. Although I was making A's in my honor classes, I began to feel like an impostor. After all, I was an honor student who made a C. Didn't that "weakest link" confess my true abilities—or lack thereof?

You've just read a variety of reasons that detail the "whys" that may be lurking behind your Impostor Syndrome. You might even be thinking, *It's so pervasive. Maybe I should just . . . accept it.*

As your coach, allow me a single, important word on this: "*No!*"

One of my mentors suggested to me that our lives are roughly made of up "thirds":

- 1/3 our genetics

- 1/3 our environment

- 1/3 our choices

You didn't decide who your parents would be or where you would grow up. However you *do* have control to make your own choices in life.

Take Adam and Eve's story. They did not have a say in who their Father was. They did not have a say in their environment (the Garden of Eden itself!). However, they did have free will to choose if they would or would not eat the forbidden fruit. Regrettably, they decided to disobey God, which resulted in a much harsher life for all of humanity.

Choices matter.

So don't stop here. I'm about to focus on actions to help you at last overcome Impostor Syndrome—part of the force that's been handcuffing you, and some of those good works God has for you!

You'll be one decision away from having a different mindset about your life.

The "maximizer" in me is rooting for you. You've got this!

....

*"I'm not a classic impostor-syndrome person—
because I have that initial insecurity, but I'm
capable of stepping outside of it and
proving to myself it's wrong."*

–Justice Sonia Sotomayor,
U.S. Supreme Court Justice

....

PART 4

. . . .

Bye, Impostor Syndrome!

What triggers your impostor's entry? It might be the concern of possible failure. Being overlooked or underestimated. Missing an opportunity to speak your mind—or someone else stating the same idea first. Failing to be recognized for your efforts. Saying something dumb in a meeting. Your answer to "what do you do for a living?" falling short of what you'd pictured. Talking with a classmate from high school, or that person whom you always feel insecure.

My Impostor Syndrome would be also provoked during my time as a sign language interpreter at my church.

When I was about 9 years old, I learned the sign language alphabet from a book and I recalled it to the age of 31. During this time, my church was participating in the *The Purpose Driven Life* church study by Rick Warren. I began to wonder what was my personal ministry? I was thinking, *"You are always watching the church interpreter maybe that is your ministry?"* As I pondered the idea, some of my limiting beliefs began popping to the forefront. *"You're pregnant, you don't have time to learn something new!.. You can't just introduce yourself to a stranger!.. How can you be a part of a ministry and you only know the alphabet?"* Thankfully I pushed past those and within three months I signed my first sermon.

A few months later, I decided to venture out alone outside the comforting walls of my church and attend the homecoming game at the local school for the Deaf. As I interacted with the people attending the game, I began to feel way over my head, incompetent even. They were signing words I had never seen and at a pace that was far faster than what I was accustomed to. After discovering I was hearing, they would graciously slow down the speed of their hands or explain the meaning of the words.

As time progressed, my skills improved. Although, I was considered an effective interpreter by our Deaf and ministry members. I began to notice my uncomfortable feeling deepened and thoughts persisted about my interpreting skills...

"I still can't believe they're letting me do this!... It's only a matter of time before they find out....I fooled

them again...I don't know how I pulled that off."

Again, I didn't know what I was experiencing had a name—Impostor Syndrome. You may be in the the same situation right now as I was back then.

Congratulations! By reading this book, you have begun your journey to self-discovery. This guidebook will help you develop and execute a battle plan to combat and overcome your Impostor Syndrome.

Let's get started!

11 Coach Felicia Requests to Overcome Impostor Syndrome

1. Give your Impostor Syndrome personality a name.

I want you to make Impostor Syndrome personal. I want you to give that voice inside your head a name. That's right. Give her a name. Why?

In his book, *The Inner Game of Tennis: The Classic Guide to the Mental Side of Peak Performance*, Tim Gallwey writes that everyone has two selves. The Self 1, in all of us is the "teller". *You just slam-dunked the competition.* Or, *What were you thinking? You should have your tail between your legs.* Alternatively, Self 2, is the "doer". The "teller" does not trust the "doer" in you, despite all the "doer's" experiences, successes, and proven ability to do something. Self 1 is a complainer and condemns and undermines the confidence of Self 2.

You're probably ahead of me here: The inner "teller" standing over there in the corner of your mind berating you is your impostor.

Remember when your parents would call you by your full government name? That got your attention, right? To name something is to identify it. In calling your impostor by her name, you begin to identify the impostor in your head. *She isn't telling the truth. She is such a buzz kill. She is totally not appreciating what you've managed to achieve.* Naming her mentally awakens you to listen and pay attention to the characteristics of your impostor. You're volitionally labeling what you'll listen to, and what's just a bunch of deprecating talk.

The style of name you chose for your impostor is totally up to you. Just make it something that will awaken you to the fact that your impostor has entered the space—it is your choice whether or not to agree and act on her (brash, timid, self-deprecating, or defensive) opinions.

Mine is named "Falisha" and when she gets to talkin' crazy, I get to smirk and say "Bye, Falisha!"

Write your impostor's name here:

How can you tell when she's talking?

What are some of the recurring things she says to you?

What is your typical negative self-talk like?

2. Explore your emotional intelligence.

....

"Know thyself."

–Socrates

....

A great edge to overcoming Impostor Syndrome is understanding your Emotional Intelligence (EQ). EQ is simply the freedom to manage your thoughts, feelings, and actions. It shapes our self-awareness and the way we interact with others, guides how and what we learn, and makes priority setting a possibility.

Emotional intelligence is directly associated with your professional and personal success. People with a high degree of emotional intelligence make more money than people with a low degree of emotional intelligence—an average of $29,000 more per year! And get this: EQ is the driving force behind 58 percent of all advancement across all professions.

Emotional intelligence differs from IQ in that IQ is thought to be set fairly early in an individual's life—while EQ can be developed over time.

Higher EQ lends itself to improved decision making, leadership, reading the emotions in others, and engaging in a greater number of mutually beneficial workplace outcomes.

The five components of EQ are:

1. Self-awareness

2. Self-recognition

3. Motivation

4. Empathy

5. Social Skills

Before you can have self-improvement—overcoming this beast of Impostor Syndrome crouching on your shoulder—you have to first be self-aware. (It can be difficult to recognize at first.)

Self-awareness entails understanding your needs, traits, habits, wants, desires, and blind spots. The more you perform self-introspection, understand your emotions, and what makes you tick, the easier your self-improvement will be. Self-awareness will empower you to make changes that will build on your strengths and identify skills you want to further develop. Or as G.I. Joe says, "Now you know--and knowing is half the battle." Psychologist Daniel Goleman, author of the best-selling book *Emotional Intelligence*, proposed self-awareness as "*knowing one's internal states, preferences, resources and intuitions.*" His definition includes our ability to monitor our inner thoughts and emotions as they occur.

According to Six Seconds[10], *emotions* are chemicals released in the body because of a specific trigger.

---

[10]http://www.6seconds.org/2017/05/14/emotion-feeling-mood/

We have many emotions in a day, each derived from situations and last for about six seconds.

Remember Disney's animated movie, *Inside Out*? The story is about Riley, a young girl whose world is shaken when her family moves from Minnesota to San Francisco. But the entire film is played out within Riley's mind, through the "characters" of her emotions: Joy, Sadness, Anger, Fear, and Disgust. The main storyline shows how you can detect different emotions and yet work with other emotions at the same time.

Each of us, as you can see, possess an intricate, intimate web of triggers. Do you know your emotional triggers?

If you were to form an emotional graph or diary of your day...when do you have your most angry or emotional moments? What signals your emotions to take over? This can offer us a fantastic visual for which emotion is at the "controls" of our minds.

For me, I sense disgust and anger seizing control of me when I encounter someone being patronizing or not being genuine (dare I say phony?). There's something about that fake attitude that makes me feel "emotional."

Did you notice that four out of the five primary emotions—joy, sadness, anger, fear, and disgust—could be viewed as "negative?"

The question is merely what will you do with those emotions. Each obviously has its purpose—even anger, which can motivate us to set injustices aright. Explore these Scriptures that tell of Jesus showing his emotions:

Jeremiah 32:41 - *"I will rejoice in doing them good, and I will plant them in this land in faithfulness, with all my heart and all my soul."*

John 11:35 - *"Jesus wept."*

Matthew 21:12 - *"And Jesus entered the temple and drove out all who sold and bought in the temple, and he overturned the tables of the money-changers and the seats of those who sold pigeons."*

Matthew 26:38 - *"Then he said to them, "My soul is very sorrowful, even to death; remain here, and watch with me."*

Matthew 20:34 - *"And Jesus in pity touched their eyes, and immediately they recovered their sight and followed him."*

Through consistent choices, you can also develop your skills to *respond* logically and wisely rather than *react* emotionally to things. The Bible cautions, *"take every thought captive to obey Christ."* (2 Corinthians 10:5) If we're not capturing negative thoughts and reining them in with truth, they actually change our brains to be more susceptible in the future. An unknown author wrote: *"Practice the pause. When in doubt, pause. When angry, pause. When tired, pause. When stressed, pause. And when you pause, pray!"*

3. Remove Your Limiting Beliefs.

•••••••••••••••••••

"You have the power in the present moment to change limiting beliefs and consciously plant the seeds for the future of your choosing. As you change your mind, you change your experience."

–Serge King, *author*

•••••••••••••••••••

Many times you filter information based on what you believe. Limiting beliefs are deep-rooted ideas you have about yourself that you accept without questioning. For example:

"I don't have the skills."

"I don't have time."

"I'm not deserving of this success."

"I was just not born with that ability."

"I can't go any further."

"I'm not creative."

"I don't have the will power."

"I can't connect with people."

"I just don't speak well."

"I'm not smart."

"That's just not my personality."

"I'm not mechanically inclined."

"Other people can do it better than me."

"I don't know enough."

"I'm not an expert."

"I'm too old…. too young."

"I can't because I have kids."

"I don't know what I want."

"What is meant to be will be."

Did one of those hit home with you? Sometimes we live with limiting beliefs put on us by others. They make you play small instead of big. They can make you avoid situations that could be great for you. They make you miss wonderful opportunities. Limiting beliefs hold you back!

"The Fleas and Invisible Lid" is a story[11] about a scientist exploring limiting beliefs and perceptions. In the experiment, a scientist placed a number of fleas in a glass jar. They quickly jumped out. He then put the fleas back into the jar and placed a glass lid over the top. The fleas began jumping and hitting the glass lid, falling back down into the jar. After a while, the fleas, conditioned to the presence of the glass lid, began jumping slightly below the glass lid so as not to hit it. The scientist then removed the glass lid as it

---

[11]https://www.ziglar.com/product/biscuits-fleas-and-pump-handles/

was no longer needed to keep the fleas in the jar. The fleas learned to limit themselves from jumping beyond the height of the lid. even if the lid was removed—shall we call it the glass ceiling, ladies?—they were conditioned to the "fact" that they cannot escape from the jar.

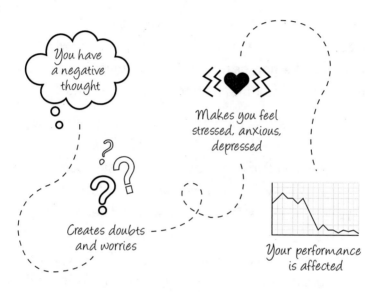

You have a negative thought

Creates doubts and worries

Makes you feel stressed, anxious, depressed

Your performance is affected

Limiting beliefs are usually attached to past emotions and experiences. Are you limiting yourself in what you can achieve based on your past?

Maybe you're thinking, Coach, *how do I know if it's a limiting belief—or just something that's true about me?*

Good question. And that's the real kicker of this whole syndrome, isn't it? A limiting belief is one that keeps us from even exploring what God might have outside the teensy box of our thinking. Take a look at David and Goliath (1 Samuel 17). David didn't feel his size was limiting, or his lack of expertise or armor. His faith was in his God—not in his résumé.

So as you look at your beliefs, assess "soberly": *Yes, I'm good at that. Nope, not good at that—but that doesn't mean God can't use it.*

To think of ourselves as God sees us: no greater, no less. I don't need to think "I'm okay" based on whether I can be like her, or not embarrass anyone, or reach my goals. Pastor and author Tim Keller writes,

> As long as you think that there is a pretty good chance you will achieve some of your dreams, as long as you think you have a shot at success, you experience your inner emptiness as "drive" and your anxiety as "hope"...Most of us keep telling ourselves that the reason we remain unfulfilled is because we simply haven't been able to achieve our goals. And so we can live almost our entire lives without admitting to ourselves the depth of our spiritual thirst.[12]

So we can look at ourselves accurately: not self-deprecating (*"I'm only a ..." "I'm not that, so I don't matter"*). Not ego-inflated. Instead, asking God who He's made us to be.

It can be strikingly difficult to untangle the subtle lies from the "tapes" that have played in our heads. Let

---

[12]*Encounters with Jesus Series: The Insider and the Outcast.* New York: Penguin Group (2013).

me show you how this works. Ready? Recently I had a limiting belief of "I can't write a book."...*for real.*

Poet and civil rights activist Maya Angelou published seven autobiographies, three books of essays, several books of poetry, and was credited with a list of plays, movies, and television shows spanning over 50 years. Despite her overwhelming success—particularly considering the vast obstacles of her time—she was quoted as saying, "*I have written eleven books, but each time I think, 'Uh oh, they're going to find out now. I've run a game on everybody, and they're going to find me out.*"

Now, I'm no Maya Angelou. But can we agree that Impostor Syndrome has no regard for achievement?

Let's unpack how I tackled my limiting belief.

Felicia's Limiting Belief: "I can't write a book."

Acknowledge it. Falisha is here. She just said I can't write a book. (Her hands were kind of on her hips, and she was giving me that look Mama gave me when I was six, dressed like Wonder Woman, and intending to fly off the bed.)

Feel it. I'm frustrated I have this belief. But I also have a sneaking suspicion she's right—so I've got that gnawing anxiety that kind of nibbles at my stomach.

Explore it. Well, I'm not a writer by occupation. But I know I have things to say.

Cross-examine it. Hmm. Well, I've never tried to write a book before... I have written numerous papers when I was a student. I usually received A's on my papers. I like researching and presenting topics with an engaging perspective. There are different styles of writing and types of books. I can write what I want—and I don't have to do this on my own.

Envision it. I can write a book to encourage others. A book to help coach people that may not be able to connect with me in person. Who knows whose lives I could touch? I can list "author" as a new title on my resume and LinkedIn profile. (Hey! I'm starting to like the sound of this.)

Choose it. I will write my book in my style. That means--bye Falisha!

Take action. I did. You're reading it now.

I have looked to scriptures for encouragement in overcoming limiting beliefs. What we perceive as limitations or handicaps or ordinariness are just what God had in mind to take our breath clean away while we watch Him do something God-sized. Here are a few scriptures that may be encouraging to you:

You say: 'It's impossible'
God says: All things are possible (Luke 18:27)

You say: 'I'm too tired'
God says: I will give you rest (Matthew 11:28-30)

You say: 'I can't go on'
God says: My grace is sufficient (2 Corinthians 12:9 & Psalm 91:15)

You say: 'I can't figure things out'
God says: I will direct your steps (Proverbs 3:5-6)

You say: 'I can't do it'
God says: You can do all things (Philippians 4:13)

You say: 'I'm not able'
God says: I am able (2 Corinthians 9:8)

You say: 'It's not worth it'
God says: It will be worth it (Roman 8:28)

You say: 'I can't forgive myself'
God says: I Forgive you (1 John 1:9 & Romans 8:1)

You say: 'I can't manage'
God says: I will supply all your needs (Philippians 4:19)

You say: 'I'm afraid'
God says: I have not given you a spirit of fear (2 Timothy 1:7)

You say: 'I'm always worried and frustrated'
God says: Cast all your cares on Me (1Peter 5:7)

You say: 'I'm not smart enough'
God says: I give you wisdom (1 Corinthians 1:30)

I want you to begin discovering and breaking down your limiting beliefs. First...

Acknowledge it. Recognize that your impostor self has entered the scene and is talking crazy. What's the snippet of truth she says? What lies are mixed in? Think about the limiting beliefs you hold today and write them down.

Feel it. How do those beliefs make you feel?

Explore it. Why do these thoughts have such power over you? From whom did you first hear them? What has reinforced their validity? Was that experience valid and wise, or did you allow your misinterpretation of truth to handicap you?

Cross exam it. What actual evidence do you have that supports those beliefs? Do you just think it out of habit or is it fact?

Envision it. What could you have or accomplish by rejecting these beliefs?

Choose it. Determine which one you prefer to have long term: the limiting belief, or the vision? (Note: Sometimes we have to rework our vision so that it honestly reflects our circumstances. If I've got a disabled son at home and have my GED, it's unlikely I'll be getting my Master's degree in two years. But that doesn't mean my vision must be discarded. It might just need to be adjusted.)

Take action. What action steps will you take to make your vision reality?

4. Gather Feedback From Others.

. . . .

"Whether you think you can,
or you think you can't—you're right."

–Henry Ford, *founder of Ford Motor Company*

. . . .

Why is feedback such a vital element in your personal and career development? Because none of us have a 360°. We've all experienced how blind we can be to our own weaknesses and failures—and we've all been unaware of the ways we're valuable to our world. Sometimes we raise the level of our own treadmill, adding stress and pressure, simply because we anticipate others' disapproval.

The Johari Window, created by psychologists Joseph Luft and Harrington Ingham, is a great simple technique to derive feedback from others and uncover more about your innate strengths.

This exercise will increase your awareness of relationships you have with yourself and others—EQ, remember?

First, review this list of adjectives. Circle those you believe describe you.

- able
- accepting
- adaptable
- bold
- brave
- calm
- caring
- cheerful
- clever
- complex
- confident
- dependable
- dignified
- empathetic
- energetic
- extroverted
- friendly
- giving
- happy
- helpful
- idealistic
- independent
- ingenious
- intelligent
- introverted
- kind
- knowledgeable
- logical
- loving
- mature
- modest
- nervous
- observant
- organized
- patient
- powerful
- proud
- quiet
- reflective
- relaxed
- religious
- responsive
- searching
- self-assertive
- self-conscious
- sensible
- sentimental
- shy
- silly
- spontaneous
- sympathetic
- tense
- trustworthy
- warm
- wise
- witty

Next, select at least two people and ask them to do the same. (Become a member on my website—fsocareercoach.com—to have access to an electronic document you can send to others to complete.

Ask people that are familiar with you. People you can consider asking are:

- Your manager, colleagues, or direct reports at work.

- A close family member.

- A friend who is honest and capable of giving difficult to hear feedback.

- A mentor.

- A church group member.

- Ultimately select people that can provide meaningful feedback to you.

List some trustworthy friends, coworkers, etc., who you could invite to offer this kind of feedback to you consistently and as they see opportunities?

Collect all the lists of adjectives.

Let's discuss the layout of the window. The left side deals with things you know about yourself and the right side highlights things that you don't know about yourself. Johari Windows are not meant to be evenly shaped. Strive to expand your open area by reducing the Unknown and Blind Spot boxes, resulting in greater knowledge of yourself. Voluntarily disclosing hidden box content can result in greater interpersonal connections and friendships. If several people participated in this activity on your behalf, you can place a number by an adjective that occurs multiple times, indicating its frequency.

OPEN

cheerful
logical
organized

known to self
known to others

BLIND

confident
powerful
self-conscious

unknown to self
known to others

tense
independent
religious

known to self
unknown to others

spontaneous
searching
complex

unknown to self
unknown to others

HIDDEN **UNCONSCIOUS**

The Open

Place adjectives that are selected by both you *and* others here. This area consists of what you know about yourself and what others know about you.

What traits are "classic" you in a nutshell— unsurprising core traits?

In what circumstances do these traits really shine?

If within our greatest strength is often our greatest weakness, how can these positive traits occasionally manifest in their correlating weakness? (e.g. "I'm often confident and poised, but occasionally can be perceived as arrogant...or even be arrogant and unteachable, not listening well.")

The Blind

Place adjectives *only selected by others and not by you here*. This area represents what you don't know about yourself and what others see in you that you're not aware of.

You can "decrease" this box by continually asking people for feedback on your behaviors and attitudes. Hearing constructive criticism may be difficult at first, but is helpful in exposing possible blind spots and leads to your self-improvement.

Do you agree with the traits others selected? (Why or why not?)

What could you do to be more approachable in this respect?

How could you capitalize on these traits and explore their possibilities?

The Hidden

Adjectives *selected only by you are placed here.* This area represents what you know about yourself but choose to hide from others or only communicate when you are comfortable.

You can decrease this box by sharing more of yourself.

Why do you choose to suppress these traits? Is it intentional or unintentional?

In your past experiences, what feedback have you received (intentional or otherwise) that influences your suppression of certain traits?

The Unconscious

Adjectives *not selected by you or others go here.* This area contains things that nobody knows about you, including yourself. So perhaps rather than an area of "what/who I'm not," this box can represent "potential areas of development."

You can "decrease" this box by discovering yourself, trying new things, and using untapped skills and resources. You can also minimize this area by paying attention to your feelings (there's that EQ again!), as well as triggers that may prevent you from exercising a certain trait, paralyze you, wire this trait with a past negative experience, etc.

Which of these traits do you wish would mostly described you?

Which would be easiest to develop? Which would be most challenging?

Who do you admire as a role model for these traits? Who might be able to mentor you in their development?

Of these, which do you not care to be? Who, or what experiences, do you associate with this trait?

How would you draw your boxes based on the feedback you received? What can you do to expand your boxes?

Which of these adjectives are most surprising, and which are most exciting?

5. Create Your Own Highlight Reel

....

"Your personal brand is what differentiates you from others."

–Unknown

....

Remember the cross-examine step of addressing your limiting beliefs? Reviewing evidence of your accomplishments is a great way to not just quiet, but methodically put the kibosh to your impostor-self, creating new ingrained patterns. It will help reaffirm truth—and keep you from wallowing in self-doubt.

Ideas for your highlight reel:

- E-mails that have encouraged you

- Index cards where you've written meaningful compliments, encouragements, affirmations, and milestones, as well as their source

- Greeting cards from those who care about you

- A written log/timeline of accomplishments you want to remember—which you regularly maintain

- Comments on blogs/articles you've written

- Photographs reminding you of meaningful moments and events

- Tickets, certificates, etc. from trainings and continuing education, including their notes

- Saved voicemails from affirming colleagues, friends, clients, supervisors, and relatives

- Recommendations, including those from sites like LinkedIn

- Your résumé or CV

- Performance reviews

- Social media posts

Save your electronic or hard copy collection in a location that you can easily access. When you receive new recognition from your clients, supervisor, and friends, be sure to add it to your success file.

What are some successes you want to place in your highlight reel?

In addition, don't be afraid to display some of your accomplishments in your workspace where others can view it too. It's a visual reminder to you and others that you were—and are—successful at something.

6. Create a Playlist of Songs.

. . . .

*"One good thing about music,
when it hits you, you feel no pain."*

–Bob Marley, *singer-songwriter*

. . . .

A great song can motivate you and help you snap out of self-doubt. No, it's not an enduring fix—but it might be able to snag that funk that's bucking you by the horns and wrestle it to the ground, so you can focus on what's true, and on what God has truly empowered you to do.

Songs help remind us of who we are; of whose we are. *For we are his workmanship, created in Christ Jesus for good works, which God prepared beforehand, that we should walk in them* (Ephesians 2:10).

The word "walk" reminds me of baseball players and their "walk up" songs. A walk up song would give identity to the batter who is approaching the plate and was meant to pump up the player. Often athletes use songs to motivate them to excel at their task at hand. My son, Gabriel, has been playing baseball since he was five. He gets to select what songs we listen to on the way to games or practices. We listen to songs that get him excited, focused, and ready to play well.

Yes, his mama has a playlist too! Here are a few

songs that have inspired me. You may like some of these as well:

"New Attitude" by Patti Labelle

"Am I Wrong" by Nico & Vinz (See? Don't confine yourself to artists of your own gender!)

"Declaration (This Is It)" by Kirk Franklin

"My Day" by Canton Jones

"The Comeback" by Danny Gokey

"You're the Best" by Joe Esposito

"I Don't Get Tired" – Kevin Gates

"The Glow" (anthem from *The Last Dragon*) by Willie Hutch

What's your "pre-game warm up" routine for those tasks or days that seem bigger than you are?

List songs that make you feel that vibe of confidence.

Start building your playlist today! Then rock out to it often or as needed.

7. Project Your Power.

. . . .

"Our bodies change our minds,
and our minds can change our behavior,
and our behavior can change our outcomes."

–Amy Cuddy, *speaker*

. . . .

Would you believe me if I told you that you could often spot your impostor-self from a mile—no, a desk— away?

Recently, I was scheduled to attend a meeting held around a standard conference room table: single chairs at the head, and additional chairs flanking the sides. I arrived to the room at the same time as a few of my female coworkers; there were no males in the room yet. As they filed in, I was amazed to see, one by one, each avoiding seats they viewed as for the leaders. All of them then sat quietly with their hands in their laps and a slight body slouch. As I chose my seat at the head of the table with my head held erect, I couldn't help but to wonder: Did my colleagues understand the nonverbal cues they were giving off?

Your posture is a strong indicator of your confidence level. Studies have shown that how we move and hold our bodies affects our thought patterns.[13] *It even*

---

[13]The author acknowledges controversy surrounding these studies; see http://fortune.com/2016/10/02/power-poses-research-false/ and http://ideas.ted.com/inside-the-debate-about-power-posing-a-q-a-with-amy-cuddy/

affects how other people perceive us. We can use our bodies to increase confidence and performance by striking a power pose. Researcher Amy Cuddy observes,

> *As Columbia University professor Adam Galinsky and colleagues wrote in a 2016 review, a person's "sense of power . . . produces a range of cognitive, behavioral, and physiological consequences," including improved executive functioning, optimism, creativity, authenticity, the ability to self-regulate and performance in various domains, to name a handful.*[14]

View the two poses below. What do you feel she is communicating to others with each pose?

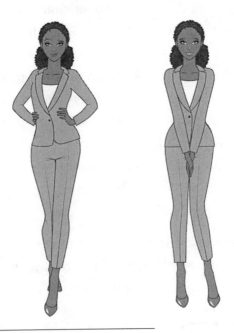

---

[14]http://ideas.ted.com/inside-the-debate-about-power-posing-a-q-a-with-amy-cuddy/

When your impostor-self shows up or you are experiencing self-doubt, I want you to notice the position your body is in at the time. Are you hunched over at your desk? Are you standing with your head bowed? Are you touching your neck? Are you shrinking yourself in some fashion?

Remember, when your impostor-self shows up, first acknowledge her presence by name. Then begin placing your body in a power pose. Let your impostor know you are in charge.

1. If you're sitting, simply raise your chest and hold your head up.

2. Steepling: Place your fingertips together in front of you and push your hands apart.

3. Wonder Woman: Stand tall with your chest out and your hands on your hips. (There's a reason we see superheroes in a power pose!)

4. While standing, place hands a little bit more than shoulder width apart and spread finger tips apart and push down on table.

5. Sitting or standing, place your arms behind

your head. This can communicate ease and confidence with the situation—though consider avoiding it for more formal meetings in which you need to convey poise.

6. If you're alone, try the Victory Stance: Plant your feet widely and stretch your arms overhead in a V shape. Lift your head and gaze at the ceiling. (I often think of giving praise to God while doing this one.)

Take your posing to the next level by playing your power playlist in the background.

You may be thinking, *Really, Coach Felicia? That seems weird.* I know, but it works! Studies have shown that these poses boost abstract thinking, helping people perform better in interviews or before a test, and decrease stress hormones by 25 percent.[15]

---

[15]http://www.doctoroz.com/slideshow/power-these-5-poses

8. Take care of your whole person.

. . . .

"I felt that I had so much to prove. I felt like I had to be the person who answered emails the fastest, stayed up the latest, and worked the hardest... The advice I would give any woman going into the job if she has a sense of Impostor Syndrome would be: There will be nothing if you don't look out for you."

–Lena Dunham, *director*

. . . .

Research has shown poor health and a lack of wellness supports negative emotions—and vice versa.[16] Exercising, relaxing, and eating a balanced diet can help increase your confidence level and overall sense of well-being. As a bonus, you'll be more resilient and able to respond from a sense of wholeness to situations of adversity or frustration.

You may be thinking, *I don't have time to exercise, meditate, take a lunch break... I can't drink 8 cups of water a day, because then I'll have to go to the bathroom all the time..... I'm busy being productive.*

Okay, I hear you. Let's look at this old school story about a young woodcutter who asks a logging crew foreman for a job.

---

[16]For more information, explore articles such as http://thescienceexplorer. com/brain-and-body/mind-body-connection-new-evidence-how-mental-states-alter-organ-function and https://www.ncbi.nlm.nih.gov/pmc/articles/PMC1456909/

"Let's see you cut this tree first," said the foreman.

The young man stepped forward and skillfully cut down the large tree. The foreman was impressed and said to the young man, "You can start on Monday."

Monday, Tuesday and Wednesday came and went. On Thursday afternoon the foreman came to the young man and said, "You can pick up your paycheck on your way out today."

Startled the young man exclaimed, "But I thought you paid on Friday!"

"That's right," said the foreman, "but we are letting you go today because you have fallen behind. Our daily production charts show that you have dropped from first place to last place."

"But I work really hard," said the young man. "I arrive early, I leave late and I even work through my breaks. Please don't just fire me."

The foreman knew he was telling the truth, because he had been observing him. Then he asked: "Have you been sharpening your axe?"

The young man replied: "No sir. I have been working too hard to take time for that."

· · · · · · · · · · · · · · · · · · · ·

"If the iron is blunt, and one does not sharpen the

edge, he must use more strength, but wisdom helps one to succeed."

–Ecclesiastes 10:10

. . . .

Stop and sharpen your axe!

Make sure you participate in some form of exercise you naturally enjoy! You've got enough that's uphill in your life. You need to slide exercise into the "me time" category. That is to say, rather than making exercise another, potentially overwhelming "have to", how can you create positive associations with exercise and view it as something that fuels you? If you hate running, don't decide your form of exercise has to be running in the mornings. Your commitment to it will fade quickly.

I like to dance so I enjoy participating in hip-hop dance aerobic classes. Maybe your thing is spin class, Zumba, step aerobics, walking, boot camp, water aerobics, chopping wood . . . simply make a commitment to do it regularly. (And consider adding your playlist!) Regular exercise offers tangible increases in your energy levels and emotional health.

Rest, too, is critical to your health—and more of that viewing yourself with "sober judgment," submitting to God's rhythms for your life. You're not a "human doing"—you're a human being. Repeat after me: *My value does not hinge on my ability to work, produce, and achieve.* I like how author and entrepreneur Tsh Oxenreider puts it: *"No matter where I am or what roles I've been given, the point of my life is not usefulness, but in knowing God and enjoying Him forever."*

Does the essence of your life constantly have you on the go? You'll probably always have something pressing that needs to be done—the tyranny of the urgent. But like the woodsman, people may see you working, but are you really producing. Replenish. Rest. Refresh. Take mental pauses. *Enjoy.*

Again, sharpen your axe!

Not sure where to start? Start with this streamlined 3-2-1 Silence Plan:

Daily – 3 minutes of silence

Weekly – 2 hours of solitude

Monthly – 1 day of retreat

What area of your holistic health is the most neglected: physical, emotional, social, intellectual, spiritual, occupational, financial, or environmental?

How would those closest to you answer that question?

What are two action points you could commit to in order to nurture your most lacking aspects of holistic health?

9. Promote Yourself Confidently.

....

"Self-promotion is a leadership and political skill that is critical to master in order to navigate the realities of the workplace and position you for success."

–Bonnie Marcus, *author*

....

Picture it. You're at a professional event, lanyard swinging, and binder beneath your arm. Another attendee walks up to you. You shake hands, exchange names, and she then asks you that killer question: "What is it that you do?"

Introducing yourself is more than just offering your name and title. You want to share how you contribute or serve other people. Here is an example of how I may introduce myself at an event:

Tamika: Hi. I'm Tamika Lewis.

Felicia: Hi. I'm Felicia Johnson.

Tamika: Nice to meet you Felicia. What do you do?

Felicia: Actually, I help people stop feeling like a fraud and flourish in their careers.

Tamika: Okay… interesting. How do you do that?

Felicia: A lot of successful people have difficulty owning their success. They have thoughts like,

I'm a fraud, I don't belong, I have to be twice as good. It's known as Impostor Syndrome, and it highly affects women and minorities. So I offer coaching services to help them overcome that self-doubt and critic within themselves.

Tamika: Really? Is that what it's called? We need to talk more!

And the connection begins. When we're courageous enough to tactfully, gently, and confidently communicate about ourselves, we may fling doors open to greater opportunities.

Are you ready to confidently introduce yourself and share what you do?

Let's practice. Envision the same scenario and verbally speak out loud your introduction. (Remember your body language. Are you looking down or slumping?)

How did you do? Did you find it difficult to concisely describe what you do?

Unfortunately, this is one of the visible areas where women downplay their skills. I've personally heard many women use the words "*just*", "*only*", and "*little*" when describing themselves. We hedge our words, as if we had something to minimize. Did you use any of those words when you practiced?

Don't let your impostor get in the way. You need to be comfortable with self-promotion. Michael Hyatt, former CEO of Thomas Nelson Publishers, writes in his post, "Everything You Fear about Platforms is Wrong,"

> *A platform amplifies what you are. If you're humble, helpful, and kind, a platform won't turn you into a Me Monster. It'll enable you to leverage more of what drives you—and your humility, helpfulness, and kindness will have an even greater impact....*

> *When Ezra needed to communicate the Law of Moses to the Israelites, he didn't try doing it standing amongst the crowd. Instead, he stood on a literal platform so he could be heard. It would have actually been more self-centered if he feigned humility and spoke so people couldn't hear...*

> *All [media uses] are susceptible to pride and ego, too. But that doesn't mean we should avoid them. It means we should get over ourselves and serve others—and that's happening every day.*

Self-promotion doesn't have to be arrogant. We can keep in mind God's words—"*What do you have that you did not receive? If then you received it, why do you boast as if you did not receive it?*"—and still use what we've been given to further invest those gifts (1 Corinthians 4:7)

Practice how you introduce yourself to others. Create a one sentence curiosity statement that engages your listener to want to know more about you. You don't need something that sounds like a infomercial. And obviously there's a place for every introduction; this one might be a little out of place, say, at church. Yours should be a confident, unimposing version of how you serve.

Start with questions like these:

What do you do that is valuable to others?

What do you love most about your job?

What might people find interesting and unexpected about what you do?

Build your statement into a conversational introduction that helps people understand how you serve others.

- What about social media... For example, LinkedIn.

- Do you have a professional picture of yourself?

- Did you take the time to fill in your current and former employment positions?

- LinkedIn is a great tool which allows you to promote yourself to others.

- A great way to see how others perceive you is to ask for written recommendations.

10. Pause and say "thank you".

Center of American Progress hosted Leveraging the Power of Black Women and one of the speakers was Susan Taylor. She is an African American women who is an editor, writer, and journalist. She served as editor-in-chief of Essence Magazine and in 1994, American Libraries referred to Taylor as "the most influential Black woman in journalism today."

When they began the Q&A session after her presentation, another woman, Marcia, stood up and asked her this question.[17]

> **Marcia:** *"My name is Marcia and you speak with a lot of authority and for someone just starting her career and who also wants to make change, is there any advice for me or anybody in the room really?"*

> **Susan:** *[with a questioning tone] "Well... I sound like someone that speaks with authority? Interesting, you don't see the insecurities we all have? You know I was terrified today. I am always terrified before I speak. It makes you do your homework and think critically about what you're going to say and not, you know...*

> [she stops talking, takes a deep breath and refocuses]

> *Okay, what I wanted to say, what I would say to all you young women is buy property."*

Did you hear her impostor show up?

Remember, don't downplay your contribution or your authority..."Ah, it's no big deal." "That was nothing." "It was just..."

Rather implement the pause and graciously say, "Thank you."

Pause again. Depending on the situation, you can elaborate with something like, "I enjoyed tackling that project and the results that came through."

Understand that when you reject someone's compliment you may be inadvertently insulting the person, indicating their comment is off track.

11. Provide Support and Seek Support.

....

"As iron sharpens iron,
so one person sharpens another."

–Proverbs 27:17

....

In our spiritual lives, each of us can benefit from a Paul (mentor), a Barnabas (accountability partner), and a Timothy (someone to mentor).

A survey found one of the top preventers of women becoming mentors is...wait for it...they don't believe they have the expertise.

(Did you recognize that as a limiting belief? Good!)

The Impostor Syndrome causes you to doubt what you do know and do have—your abilities to encourage, invest in, listen, and coach others. Mentoring is an active way for you to be motivated in gratitude for just how far you have come. It causes you to rehearse and remember all you've gleaned, refreshing it for even sharper use—because teaching is one of the best methods to truly internalize what we know. The best part is embracing the opportunity to change someone's life.

Who knows? Maybe you'll prevent the next victim of Impostor Syndrome. And that's what I call a win-win.

"Be strong, be fearless, be beautiful. And believe that anything is possible when you have the right people there to support you."

–Misty Copeland, *American ballet dancer*

One of the biggest fears of people with Impostor Syndrome is being found out. Sharing your feelings with someone you trust can help reduce the stress and strain you feel in bearing your responsibilities and living up to expectations. Now that you know, more specifically, what may be holding you back, consider seeking the advice of a mentor or coach who understands the challenges you face.

As a professional coach, I have coaches and mentors on what I like to call my "personal board of directors". I'm humbled and invigorated by how my mentor described our relationship:

Felicia contacted me when she was seeking a mentor. We have been meeting together for over a year and I have found her to be one of the most teachable people I've ever met. She is curious about life, love, spirituality, relationships in the workplace and absolutely everything else. I never know what we will talk about in our time together, but I do know that it will be interesting and informative, and the time will go quickly! Felicia is easy to talk to, very transparent with her struggles and honest about areas where she wants to grow. She is an avid learner and diligently reads each book I suggest. She takes what I say to heart, often taking notes during our conversations. We challenge and encourage one another. Our relationship has become one of mutual friendship, not just mentor/mentee and I look forward to our times together.

Sometimes finding a reliable mentor can be a challenge; in fact, according to one study, 63 percent of women have never had a formal mentor. A female executive explained, "It's like walking up to someone and asking them to be your friend, and no one does that."

If finding a mentor in your area is difficult—or if you want to speak with someone that may have more of an objective viewpoint of you—hiring a coach is a great way to get the support you need.

It can sometimes be difficult to immediately witness the benefits of investing in a coach (not unlike a coach or instructor for any other skill, right? Hiring a clarinet instructor does not automatically make you a clarinet player.) Let's look at it like this. When you walk into a department store and buy a ready-to-wear dress off the rack, you get what you immediately see in the store. The dress may be cute! But it may not be manufactured from high-quality material, tailored to fit your figure, or demonstrate unique design.

Coaching is like commissioning a custom couture dress. It's crafted from quality materials; it will flatter your figure. It's also painstakingly sewn by a master seamstress, helping you leave a powerful impression for years.

A coach will ask you to:

- Keep an open-mind, and experiment.

- Change beliefs and patterns that no longer serve you.

- Remain centered and engaged during sessions.

- Actively grow between sessions through writing, taking action, and resolving relationship issues—your "homework".

What would you look for in a great mentor or coach? List as many traits as you can think of.

What goals would you wish to accomplish with this support system in your life? Include goals that are tangible (reach a promotion), specific (within one year), and reachable.

What specific traits, inhibitors, or negative patterns would you hope to overcome?

What's most likely to get in the way of you acquiring a mentor or coach? In reality, is the benefit of that supportive relationship worth it to you to overcome these obstacles?

Who comes to mind that you could talk to? (Brainstorm here, listing as many names as you can—including those who could possibly connect you to a mentor.)

CONCLUSION

· · · · · · · · · · · · · · · · · · · ·

Impostor Syndrome wasn't developed in you overnight; it will not be overcome in a day. In some ways, it may tempt you and taint your thought patterns for decades to come. But the good news: You do have control over its reign and effects.

How much Impostor Syndrome controls your life rests in no one else's hands but yours. Be the conqueror of the Impostor—and be courageous to know your true greatness.

For now, I'll leave you with these inspiring words from Marianne D. Williamson, a spiritual activist, author, and lecturer.

Our deepest fear is not that we are inadequate.

Our deepest fear is that we are powerful beyond measure.

It is our light, not our darkness that most frightens us.

We ask ourselves, Who am I to be brilliant, gorgeous, talented, and fabulous?

Actually, who are you not to be? You are a child of God.

Your playing small does not serve the world. There is nothing enlightened about shrinking so that other people will not feel insecure around you.

We are all meant to shine, as children do.

We were born to make manifest the glory of God that is within us.

It is not just in some of us; it is in everyone and as we let our own light shine, we unconsciously give others permission to do the same.

As we are liberated from our own fear, our presence automatically liberates others.

ABOUT THE AUTHOR

Felicia M. Johnson is a Certified Life Coach who leads people in solving their pressing problems—and creating a plan of success.

Raised in a military family, she witnessed firsthand the tireless work and dedication it took to be a leader. Constantly having to move and adapt to new environments provided the foundation for her ability to problem-solve and work cross-culturally.

As a high-achieving career Black woman who is also a wife, mother, business owner, and community leader, she has combated self-doubt, sexism, and racism. Yet through continued personal investment, she discovered how to persevere toward success in her career and personal life.

Felicia specializes in helping people problem solve career, personal, or business challenges and create action plans to achieve their desired success. She also facilitates career and personal development workshops and coaches women who encounter Impostor Syndrome.

Her services include assessments, individual and group coaching, and mock interviewing.

....

"People don't want feedback; they want attention . . .
They want future-focused, individualized attention on
how to get better: they want coaching."

–Marcus Buckingham, *author*

....

Want further assistance?

Contact me today about individual coaching.

Email: me@feliciasigningoff.com
website: feliciasignignoff.com

Online Self-Assessments Also Available

Hartman Value Profile Self—Unlike many self-report assessments, this assessment objectively captures your thinking pattern.

Motivators—This values index will help you understand your motivators and drivers and how to maximize your performance by achieving better alignment and passion for what you do.

Emotional Intelligence (EIQ-2)—This assessment helps you understand the correlation between the way you apply your current EQ and the outcome of your interactions with others. This lends itself to improved decision making, leadership, reading the emotions in others and engaging in a greater number of mutually beneficial workplace outcomes.

Testimonials

"Look no further for a great career coach... She is someone that challenges you to move out of your comfort zone, but provides the encouragement to do so. Felicia is great about helping you to see blind spots...things that you overlook as "normal", but in reality are, like I said, blind spots that can potentially slow your progress. Perhaps things that you are not willing to see about yourself. Felicia's goal is to help you accomplish your goals. She is fun, thought provoking and helps you to set goals and encourages you to follow through. I'm seeing myself grow and becoming more confident."

....

"Felicia has been very knowledgeable and supportive through this entire process. If you need someone to help guide you through your different career options, she is definitely the woman for the job!"

....

"Coaching at Its Best! "My experience with Coach Felicia has been very inspiring and has helped me get clarity in my life. Felicia displays professionalism, courtesy, and compassion for others and is highly recommended."

NOTES

....